Acknowledgement of Land & of the Traditional Owners of this Land

I would like to acknowledge the Gadigal people of the Eora Nation, upon whose stolen land I stand on today.
I recognise that this land was never terra nullius — the land belonging to these peoples was never ceded, given up, bought or sold.
I would like to pay my respects to Aboriginal Elders past, present and emerging, and I extend this acknowledgement to all Aboriginal and Torres Strait Islander people.

Puff the Magic Dragon

Puff, the magic dragon lived by the sea
And frolicked in the autumn mist in a land called Honah Lee
Little Jackie Paper loved that rascal Puff
And brought him strings, and sealing wax, and other fancy stuff

Oh, Puff, the magic dragon lived by the sea
And frolicked in the autumn mist, in a land called Honah Lee
Puff, the magic dragon, lived by the sea
And frolicked in the autumn mist, in a land called Honah Lee

Together they would travel on a boat with billowed sail
Jackie kept a lookout perched on Puff's gigantic tail
Noble kings and princes would bow whenever they came
Pirate ships would lower their flags when Puff roared out his name

A dragon lives forever, but not so little boys
Painted wings and giant's rings make way for other toys
One gray night it happened, Jackie Paper came no more
And Puff, that mighty dragon, he ceased his fearless roar

His head was bent in sorrow, green scales fell like rain
Puff no longer went to play along the cherry lane
Without his lifelong friend, Puff could not be brave
So Puff, that mighty dragon, sadly slipped into his cave

Oh, Puff, the magic dragon lived by the sea
And frolicked in the autumn mist, in a land called Honah Lee
Puff, the magic dragon, lived by the sea
And frolicked in the autumn mist, in a land called Honah Lee

- "Puff The Magic Dragon"- Peter Paul & Mary
Songwriters: Robin Spielberg/Leonard Lipton/Peter Yarrow

I lie...
...and that's the "TRUTH"!
"The Don"

CONTENTS

1: Island of Lost Souls
(L'isola delle Anime Perdute)
2: Licensed to Kill
(Licenza di uccidere)
3: This is America...
(Questa è l'America...)
4: In My Time of Dyin'
(Nel Mio Tempo di Morire)
5: The Joker
(Il Burlone)
6: The Entertainer
(L'intrattenitore)
7: Stop Telling Me What to FUCKING Do!
(Smettila di Dirmi cosa Cazzo Fare!)
8: Horse with a Name
(Cavallo con un Nome)
9: Eating Kills
(Mangiare Uccide)
10: We are Killers
(Siamo Assassini)
11: The "HoG" Café
(Il Caffè "HoG")
12: The Creators
(I Creatori)
13: "Good" is in the Eye of the Beholder
("Buono" è nell'Occhio di chi Guarda)
14: Where is Your Mind?
(Dov'è la tua Mente?)
15: The Planet God Forgot
(Il Pianeta che Dio ha Dimenticato)
16: You're a Fool!
(Sei un Pazzo!)
17: Conquer the Cock
(Conquista il Cazzo)

CONTENTS

18: Mutual Appreciation Society
(Società di Mutuo Apprezzamento)
19: Pussy POWER Time
(Tempo per il Potera della Figa)
20: The LO♥E Conundrum
(L'enigma dell'Amore)
21: Traitor
(Traditore)
22: By Invitation Only!
(Solo si Invito!)
23: I LO♥E to Do Nothing!
(Adoro non fare niente!)
24: Walk Lightly into the Night
(Cammina Leggermente nella Notte)
25: Demons
(Demoni)
26: There's No Devil!
(Non c'è nessun Diavolo)
27: Blame
(Colpa)
28: Adapt or Die!
(Adattati o Muori!)
29: Valley Girl
(Ragazza della Valle)
30: Let Old Ghosts Sleep
(Lascia Dormire i Vecchi Fantasmi)
31: It's All Good
(Va Tutto Bene)
32: Renaissance Child
(Bambino Rinascimentale)
33: Perception
(Percezione)
34: Simulation
(Simulazione)

CONTENTS

35: The Pusher
(Il Pusher)
36: Art & Morality
(Arte e Morale)
37: In the "Land of the Blind"
(Nel "Paese dei Ciechi")
38: I Am a Romantic
(Sono un Romantico)
39: LO♥E Bombed
(AMORE Bombardato)
40: Wired
(Cablato)
41: Kiss My Ring
(Bacia il Mio Anello)
42: Existence
(Esistenza)
43: I Matter
(Io Sono importante)
44: She was the Best Drunk I've Ever Known
(Era la Migliore Ubriaca che abbia mai Conosciuto)
45: Screw
(Vite)
46: Wiser than Her Years
(Più Saggio dei Suoi Anni)
47: No One Comes Back
(Nessuno Torna Indietro)
48: I Have Learnt
(Ho Imparato)
49: The Earth is Burning
(La Terra sta Bruciando)
50: Internal Landscape
(Paesaggio Interno)

Island of Lost Souls

(L'isola delle Anime Perdute)

A *"Soul"*...
...do I have a *"Soul"*?
Do you have a *"Soul"*?
Do we have a *"Soul"*?
Is there such a thing as a *"Soul"*?
If there is…
...then I'm living on the...
...*"Island of Lost Souls"*.

Is your *"Soul"* here too?
Maybe my *"Soul"* will meet your *"Soul"*...
...on the *"Island of Lost Souls"*.

"Oh buccaneer
Can ya help me put my truck in gear?
Can ya take me far away from here?
Save my soul from sin?

You want to get away you've had it man
Nothing's going right
So come sit on the sands of the island
Island of Lost Souls.

No luxuries, no no amenities
Too dull, your senses
Oh oh only primitive
"Hey hey really get away" is what he said
Where did he go?
I'm tired of waiting here for him
Where can he be?
He's not with me.

Hey ya hey ya hey ya Island of Lost Souls."

- *"Island of Lost Souls"*
Performed by: Blondie
Written by: Christopher Stein/Deborah Harry

"The Don"
04.03.2023

Licensed to Kill

(Licenza di uccidere)

You are...
...*Licensed to KILL!*
...And to THRILL!

"The Don"
04.03.2023

This is America...

(Questa è l'America...)

"This is America...
...we don't share land here!"

"John Dutton owner of "Yellowstone Ranch", in the TV series
"Yellowstone"."

"The Don"
05.03.2023

In My Time of Dyin'

(Nel Mio Tempo di Morire)

I knew I was going to die from when I was about six years old.
So, the idea of death & dyin' is not something new to me.
It has been a part of my whole life.
It's not as if it suddenly sprung up on me.
It's not as if I didn't know about it.
It's not as if it took me by surprise.
It's not as if it came out of nowhere.
It's not as if it wasn't expected.
It's not something new.

Death & dyin' is everywhere.
It surrounds our very existence.
It envelopes our very being.
Everything we do is based on it.
We *fear it*.
We *deny it*.
We *try to escape it*.
We *fight it*.
But we can NEVER run away from it.
We can NEVER beat it.
And we know that.
It's just that we will NEVER accept it.
We live a life of illusion.
Stupidly seeking ways to gain immortality.
Delusional to our mortality.

We WILL die!
That is a FACT!
An undeniable FACT!
An unescapable FACT!
Face this FACT bravely & with dignity.
Do not be a coward & run away from Death.

Face it!
Confront!
Look at Death in the eyes & say...
..."I am NOT afraid of you!"
"I am NOT afraid to die!"
Be brave in front of Death!

Live your life WITHOUT fearing Death.
This is how you defeat Death!

"In my time of dying,
I want nobody to mourn
All I want for you to do is take my body home.

Well, well, well, so I can die easy.
Well, well, well, so I can die easy."

-*"In My Time of Dyin'"*
-*Traditional/Emily Wells*
Performed by: Bob Dylan

"The Don"
07.03.2023

The Joker

(Il Burlone)

I'm the Joker.
I *make fun of everything*.
I *never take anything seriously*.
I *even make fun of myself*.
Because...
...I'm the Joker.

People think I'm *mad*.
People think I'm *crazy*.
People think I'm *insane*.
People think I'm *an idiot*.
But...
...I'm the Joker.

I see *everything as a game*.
I see *everyone as fake*.
I see *situations as being hilarious*.
I see *life as a joke*.
That's why...
...I'm the Joker.

We are *lied to*.
We are *manipulated*.
We are *controlled*
We are *treated as fools*.
So...
...I am the Joker.

I *do not play their games*.
I *play my own games*.
Because...
...I am the Joker.

"'Cause I'm a picker
I'm a grinner
I'm a lover
And I'm a sinner
I play my music in the sun
I'm a joker
I'm a smoker
I'm a midnight toker
I sure don't want to hurt no one
I'm a picker
I'm a grinner
I'm a lover
And I'm a sinner
I play my music in the sun
I'm a joker
I'm a smoker
I'm a midnight toker
I get my lovin' on the run
Ooh, whoo, ooh, whoo."

-"The Joker"
-Written by: Ahmet Ertegun/Eddie Curtis/Steve Miller
-Performed by: The Steve Miller Band

"The Don"
08.03.2023

The Entertainer

(L'intrattenitore)

I HAVE to entertain!
Because...
...EVERYTHING is so FUCKING BORING!
...EVERYONE is so FUCKING BORING!
They *do nothing*.
They *say nothing*.
They *are nothing*.
They *have NOTHING to offer*.
So...
...I entertain them.
...and I entertain myself.
Because...
...I'm the Entertainer.

I *make jokes*.
I *tell stories*.
I *stir the pot*.
I *create mischief*.
I *create trouble*.
I *mock everyone*.
I *mock everything*.
I *take nothing seriously*.
I am the Entertainer.

There is *nothing else I could do*.
There is *no-one else I could be*.
I have no choice in the matter.
It is my *destiny*.
It is my *fate*.
The Universe has planned it this way...
...and there is nothing I can do about it.
So...
...*I am the Entertainer*.

"The Don"
08.03.2023

Stop Telling Me What to FUCKING Do!

(Smettila di Dirmi cosa Cazzo Fare!)

Stop telling me what to FUCKING do!
I'm sick of it.
Get off my FUCKING back!
I don't need your *FUCKING advice.*
I don't need your *FUCKING criticism.*
And I certainly DON'T need *your FUCKING approval or validation!*
I don't need you *pontificating from on high.*
You can have your own opinion, of course.
But...
...keep it to your FUCKING self.

Stop being judgemental!
You are *so FUCKING arrogant.*
You are *deluded with your own self-importance.*
You're *NOT that important!*
I don't need you!
So...
...FUCK OFF!
...and stop telling me what to FUCKING do!

"The Don"
11.03.2023

Horse with a Name

(Cavallo con un Nome)

He is called *"Mr Ed"*, (the talking horse, who was smarter than his owner, Wilber).
He is called *"Francis"*, (another talking horse).
He is called *"Phar Lap"*, (the greatest Australian racehorse that there ever was).
He is called *"Silver"*, (the Lone Ranger's white horse. "Hi Ho Silver, away").
He is called *"Trigger"*, (Roy Roger's horse)
He was called *"Champion"*, (ridden by the "Singing Cowboy" himself, Gene Autry).
He is called *"Shadowfax"*, (owned by the great wizard, Gandalf).
He is called *"Black Beauty"* (Elizabeth Tayor's beautiful Black stallion).
He is called *"Abraxas"*, (the race horse ridden by "Icarus", whom we all know, flew too close to the Sun).
He is called *"Wildfire"*, (hero of one of my favourite songs sung by Michael Murphy. A "one-hit wonder").
He is called *"Hero"*, (he belonged to the "Shadow that walks", the "Phantom").
He is called *"Tornado"* (he belonged to "Zorro").
He is called *"Pegasus"*, (the mythological "White Winged" horse, belonging to Zeus himself).
He is called *"Stormbringer"*, (made famous by "Deep Purple" in the song of the same name).
He is called *"Death"*, (FUCK, we ALL know who rides him! He has no flesh, just a skeleton! VERY SCARY!).

"You know I've been through the desert on a horse with a name.
And it felt good to be out in the rain.
In the desert, you can remember your name
'Cause there ain't no one for to give you no pain.
La la la la la la..."

-*"Horse With No Name"*
-Performed by: America
Written by: Lee Bunnell

"The Don"
12.03.2023

Eating Kills

(Mangiare Uccide)

Bread is bad.
Pasta is bad.
Pizza is bad.
Meat is bad.
Fruit is bad.
Cheese is bad.
Butter is bad.
Cream is bad.
Ice-cream is bad.
Chocolate is bad.
Fat is bad.
Sugar is bad.
Salt is bad.
Wine is bad.
Beer is bad.
All alcohol is bad
Coffee is bad
Tea is bad.
Honey is bad.
Pussy is definitely VERY bad.
In fact...
...ALL food is bad.
Do not eat!
Because...
...eating KILLS!

If you want to live a long time...
...do NOT eat!

"Because I'm fat
I'm fat, come on
You know I'm fat
I'm fat, you know it
You know I'm fat
I'm fat, come on, you know it
Who's fat?"

- "Fat"-Michael Jackson/"Weird Al' Yankovic

"The Don"
17.03.2023

We are Killers

(Siamo Assassini)

We all kill.
Every living thing kills.
But humans are the *WORST!*.
We kill *EVERYTHING!*
I *am a killer.*
You *are a killer.*
We are ALL killers.

We kill *indiscriminately.*
We kill *wantingly.*
We kill *for our own selfish appetites.*
We kill for *pleasure.*
We kill for *fun.*
We kill for *sport.*
We kill for *amusement.*
We kill for *LO♥E.*
We kill for *HATE.*
We kill for *REVENGE.*
We kill for *greed.*
We kill for *money (in fact we do anything for money).*
We kill for *POWER!*
We just LO♥E to KILL!
Hell...
...we even kill ourselves!
We are KILLERS!

"*Oh killerman where you gonna run to?*
Oh killerman where you gonna run to?
Oh killerman where you gonna run to?
All on that day!

-*Traditional*

"The Don"
17.03.2023

The "HoG" Café

(Il Caffè "HoG")

Everyone is welcome.
No matter what colour.
No matter what sex.
The doors are always open...
...24/7/365
All year round.
You know where to find us.
It's around the back.
Just a half mile from the railroad track.
At the "HoG" café.

There is always entertainment there.
Live music every night.
You can do whatever the FUCK you like.
There are no bouncers.
No one to kick you out...
...if you get unruly.
In fact, we like unruly.
FUCK, we encourage it.
At the "HoG" café.

You meet all the famous glitterati & literati there.
Elvis is there discussing political theory with *Marx & Engels*.
Mick is sharing a pussy with *Hemingway*.
Hendrix & Marianne are enjoying a *"Mars"* bar, quietly in a dark corner.
Leonard is laughing his head off at a joke that *JFK* just told him.
I think it was the one about the *"Cuban Missile Crisis"*...
...it's an oldie but a goodie.
He uses it all the time...
...guaranteed to bring the house down.
At the "HoG" café.

Come on down.
666HoG, Beelzebub Highway, Inferno.
You won't be disappointed.
There is no dress requirement.
In fact, it is preferable if you are *NAKED!*
The only requirement for entry...
...you have to be *DEAD!*
To enter the "HoG" Café!
"The House of God" Café!

"You can get anything you want at the "House of God" Café!
You can get anything you want at the "House of God" Café!
Walk right in it's around the back
Just a half a mile from the railroad track.
You can get anything you want at the "House of God" Café!
That's the "HoG" Café!"

Even GOD!

-"Alice's Restaurant Massacree"
–Performed by: Arlo Guthrie
-Written by: Arlo Guthrie/Garry Sherman

"The Don"
21.03.2023

The Creators

(I Creatori)

There is not just ONE *"Creator"*.
There are MANY *"Creators"*.
You are a *"Creator"*.
I am a *"Creator"*.
We are ALL "Creators"!

We create every day.
We can't help it.
This is what we do.
We create!
And we mainly create...
...*havoc!*

We create *disasters*.
We create *destruction*.
We create *hatred*.
We create *greed*.
We create *wars*.
We create *EVIL*.
We create *DOOM!*
We create *DEATH!*
We create *Heaven*.
We create *Hell*.
We create *the Gods*.
Because...
...*We are "Creators"!*

It was deemed by the *"Almighty"* himself...
...*"Go forth & create!"*
And that's what we do!
I am God!
You are God!
We are ALL Gods!
Because...
...*we are ALL "Creators"!*

"The Don"
21.03.2023

"Good"
is in the Eye of the Beholder
("Buono" è nell'Occhio di chi Guarda)

Am I a *"Good"* person?
Am I a *"Bad"* person?
I think I am *"Good"* person.
But maybe I'm not!
I try to be "*Good*".
My intentions are always to be a *"Good"* person.
To do *"Good"* deeds.
However, being *"Good"* can only be judged through the eyes of others.
Only another person can say whether you are a *"Good"* person or not.
And even then, one cannot be totally sure.
Are they right in their judgement?
Do they even have the right to judge me?
"Good" & *"Bad"* are just value statements anyway.
They can & do vary from one person to the next.
One person's *"Good"* is not the same as another person's *"Good"*.
One person's "Bad" is not the same as another person's *"Bad"*.
So, I guess the safe option is to believe in yourself...
...to trust your own values & beliefs & hope they will stand you strong.
All I can say is...
...good luck.

I think that I'm a *"Good"* person but...
...I could be wrong!

"You may be right
I may be crazy
Oh, but it just may be a lunatic you're looking for
Turn out the light
Don't try to save me
You may be wrong for all I know
But you may be right."

-*"You Maybe Right"* – Billy Joel

"The Don"
22.03.2023

Where is Your Mind?

(Dov'è la tua Mente?)

Where is Your Mind?
What the FUCK are you *thinking?*
What the FUCK are you *feeling?*
What the FUCK are you *doing?*
Where is your mind?

What the FUCK were you thinking?
You weren't FUCKING thinking at all?
Were you?
You were FANTASISING again!
Living in your mind again!
Where is your mind?

It's BETTER not to *have a mind.*
It's BETTER to not be *thinking at all!*
Thinking caused problems.
Having a mind causes catastrophe!

Where is your mind?
Where is your mind?
Where is your mind?
Where is your mind?

Where is his mind?

Where is her mind?

Wake up my mind!

I have no mind!
I have no mind!
I have no mind!
I have no mind!

I am MINDLESS!

"The Don"
23.03.2023

The Planet God Forgot

(Il Pianeta che Dio ha Dimenticato)

There are billions of stars in the Cosmos.
Therefore, there are trillions of billions of planets.
And God made every one!
That's right...
...he made every single one!

Of all those planets, there must be a few he has forgotten about.
Unfortunately...
...Earth *(sweet Ghia)* is one!
Abandoned & left lost in the great *"Expanse"*!
Adrift, revolving around a star in the outer perimeter of the *"Milky Way"*
galaxy.

It is suffering...
...badly!
The dominant *(apparently)* intelligent life form is humanoid.
In fact, they don't appear to be too intelligent?
They are destroying the planet & consequently, themselves!
But they seem to be too *STUPID* to see this.
The planet needs help straight away!
Help from these stupid humans!
God...
...are you there?
No answer!

It seems that planet Earth is the planet God forgot!

"The Don"
23.04.2023

You're a Fool!

(Sei un Pazzo!)

You're a FOOL, my son.
A FOOL!
Do you hear me?
A FOOL!

"The Don"
24.03.2023

Conquer the Cock

(Conquista il Cazzo)

Control your *emotions*.
Control your *passions*.
Control your *desires*.
Control your *libido*.
Control your *lust*.
Control your *sex*.
Control your *cock*.
Conquer the cock!

Freedom from *emotions*.
Freedom from *passions*.
Freedom from *desires*.
Freedom from *libido*.
Freedom from *lust*.
Freedom from *sexual needs*.
Freedom from *the cock*.
Conquer the cock!

Don't be *ruled by the cock*.
Don't be *controlled by the cock*.
Don't be *dominated by the cock*.
Don't be *seduced by the cock*.
Don't be *manipulated by the cock*.
Don't be *hypnotised by the cock*.
Don't be *mesmerised by the cock*.
Don't be *entranced by the cock*.
Don't be *enslaved by the cock*.
Conquer the cock!

Don't be *a slave to the cock!*
Conquer the cock!

Freedom from the cock.
Conquer the cock!

Don't be *ruled by the cock*.
Conquer the cock!

Conquer the cock!

"The Don"
28.03.2023

Mutual Appreciation Society
(Società di Mutuo Apprezzamento)

Tell me that I'm intellectual...
...and I'll tell you that you're intellectual.

Tell me that I'm handsome...
...and I'll tell you that you're BEAUTIFUL.

Tell me that I'm HOT...
...and I'll tell you that you're HOT.

Tell me that I'm SEXY...
...and I'll tell you that you're SEXY.

Tell me that you'd like to FUCK me...
...and I'll tell you that I'd like to FUCK you.

Tell me that you LO♥E me...
...and I'll tell you that I LO♥E you.

"The Don"
30.03.2023

Pussy POWER Time

(Tempo per il Potera della Figa)

Hey you?
Yes...
...YOU!
It's your *time.*
It's your time to take *over.*
It's your time to take *control.*
It's your time to take *charge.*
It's your time to be the *BOSS.*
It's your time to make the *RULES.*
It's your time to be in *POWER.*
Because...
...it's Pussy POWER time!

It's time for your pussy to *come out of the DARK.*
It's time for your pussy to be *EXPOSED.*
It's your time for your pussy to be *OUTSIDE.*
It's your time for your pussy to be *SEEN.*
It's time for your pussy to *shine brightly in the SUN!*
It's time for your pussy to *SPEAK.*
It's time for your pussy to *SHOUT!*
Because...
...it's Pussy POWER time!

Pussy POWER!

Pussy POWER!

Pussy POWER!

Pussy POWER!

"The Don"
03.04.2023

The LO♥E Conundrum

(L'enigma dell'Amore)

Do NOT look for LO♥E!
Let LO♥E come to YOU!

But here's the problem...
... how can it COME to me if no one GOES looking for LO♥E?

This is the "LO♥E Conundrum"!

Solve this...
...and you will LO♥ED!

"The Don
03.04.2023

Traitor

(Traditore)

You're a *traitor*!
You stabbed me in the back!
You're a *coward*.
You're *gutless*.
You're a *"2-timer"*.
You are *"2-faced"*.
You're a *liar*.
You're a *hypocrite*.
In fact, not only are you a *TRAITOR*...
...you're also an *ARSEHOLE*!

TRAITOR!
You stabbed me in the back!

TRAITOR!
You stabbed me in the back!

TRAITOR!
You stabbed me in the back!

TRAITOR!
You stabbed me in the back!

"The Don"
08.04.2023

By Invitation Only!

(Solo si Invito!)

Do you have an *invite*?
Do you have an *invitation*?
You can only enter with an *invitation*.
No *invitation*...
...NO entry!
You are NOT welcome here!
Turn around & go home...
...and wait for an *invitation*.
Although you might never get one.
So...
...don't assume you are invited.
Don't assume you are welcome.
Because...
...you will not, without an *invitation*.
So...
...you're not allowed to...
...*look,*
...*touch,*
...*kiss,*
...*fuck.*
Or…
..*.enjoy yourself here!*
This event is by invitation ONLY!
You have NO *"RIGHTS"* here!
So...
...*FUCK OFF!*
Entry & participation is by invitation ONLY!

"The Don"
11.04.2023

(Lazy) I LO♥E to Do Nothing!

((Pigro) ADORO non Fare Niente!)

I don't know if you're anything like me…
…but…
…I LO♥E to do nothing!
I *fill my days with doing nothing at all.*
I *make no plans.*
I have no *commitments.*
I have no *obligations.*
I have no *desires.*
I have no *wants.*
I have no *needs.*
I have no *desires.*
I have *absolutely nothing.*
I LO♥E it this way!

Don't ask me to do something...
...because that would ruin my day!
I might be obliged to do it.
But...
...I *won't be HAPPY!*
I *might get ANGRY*
Because...
I LO♥E to nothing!

So...
...let me enjoy my day.
And let me do nothing.
Nothing at ALL!

"I'm LAZY!
I just stay in bed.
I'm LAAAAZZZZY!
I just stay in bed.
I don't want no money.
I don't want no bread!"

"LAAAAZZZZY!"
"I just stay in bed."

"LAAAAZZZZY!"
"I just stay in bed."

   - *"Lazy"*-Deep Purple

"The Don"
11.04.2023

Walk Lightly into the Night

(Cammina Leggermente nella Notte)

Be *light of foot.*
Have *cat's eyes.*
Have a *lion's courage.*
Have a *woman's initiation.*
Be *alert like a Meerkat.*
Be as *cautious as a deer.*
Be as *invisible as an owl.*
Be as *quiet as a mouse.*
Be *as stealthy & as sneaky as a "snake in the grass.*
Be as *inquisitive as a monkey.*
As *brave as a bear.*
Be as *innocent as a new born babe.*
Be as *wonderous as stars.*
Be as *beautiful as a red rose.*
But…
…do NOT be as *cruel as a human!*
And…
…*walk lightly in the night.*

"The man by then will be at the end of his learning & almost without warning will come to the last of his enemies.
This one is the cruelest of all & the one he won't be able to defeat completely but only fight away.
This is the time when a man has no more fears, no more impatient clarity of mind, a time when all his powers are in check but also the time when he has an unyeilding desire to rest."

-*"Do Not Go Gently"*
-*"Jeannie lewis (1973),, an avant-garde Australian performance artist"*

"Do not go gentle into that good night,
Old age should burn and rave at close of day;
Rage, rage against the dying of the light."

-*"Do Not Go Gentle into that Good Night"*
-Dylan Thomas (1951)

"The Don"
12.04.2023

Demons

(Demoni)

What populates YOUR nightmares?
What wakes you up in the middle of the night in a state of TERROR & PANIC?
Is it...?
...being eaten alive by a crocodile?
...being bitten by a zombie & becoming one of the "walking dead"?
...having your blood sucked out by Dracula & turning into a vampire?
...being attacked by "Triffids" & being kept as compost & then being eaten?
...having your mind being controlled by the "Children of the Dammed"?
...attacked by "Chucky" the killer doll?
...eaten alive by a "razorback",
...turning into a cockroach as you sleep in your bed?
...being followed & touched on the shoulder by the "Grim Reaper"?
...being attacked & eaten alive by a "White Pointer" as you swim leisurely in the sea?
...crushed & swallowed by an anaconda?
...being taken into the depths of ocean by the "Kraken"?
...being torn to shreds by "The Devil's Dogs", the guards of the Gate of the Underworld", the "Gates of HELL"!
...being abducted by aliens, experimented upon & then returned to Earth but NOT the same?
...being buried & you still being alive?

What are your demons?

What wakes you up in the middle of the night covered in a cold sweat wondering, *"What the FUCK was that ALL about"?*

Whatever your demons, do not fight them...
...do NOT fight BACK!
...they will ALWAYS win!

Your demons of the night have to be dealt with in the warm light of day...
...NOT in the cold darkness of the night.
It is what happens & do in the day that feeds & creates your demons of the night.
So...
...live during the day in a way that dies not feed or create your demons of the night.

Come to terms with your demons, reconcile with them during the day so that you can sleep peacefully at night!

"The Don"
13.04.2023

There's No Devil!

(Non c'è nessun Diavolo)

*"There's no Devil!
It's just God when he's drunk!"*

-Tom waits-"Heartattack & Vine"

"The Don"
14.04.2023

Blame

(Colpa)

No one else is to *blame* for my suffering.
You are not to *blame*.
The world is not to *blame*.
I am to *blame*.
I choose to suffer.
It's not your fault.
I cannot & should not *blame* anyone else.
It is all up to me if I choose to suffer or not.
Of course, this is not necessarily a conscious choice.
The choice is most often made for by my behavioural habits.
This is how I've always responded.
It's purely mechanical.
But no one else is to *blame* for this.
This is the misjudgement we make.
Rather than to look at oneself...
...it is easier to look externally...
...to *blame* someone else...
...when we should be looking much closer to home...
...to oneself...
...internally.
Look within & you will see the problem & the solution.
Everything starts & ends within you.
No one else is to blame.
Only you are to blame!
Accept this & you will be FREE!

"The Don"
17.04.2023

Adapt or Die!

(Adattati o Muori!)

Change is *inevitable*.
Change is *unavoidable*.
Change is *all around us*.
Change is *growth*.
Change is *evolution*.
Change is *LIFE!*
Oppose Change at your own peril.
You will inevitably fail.
You will *DIE!*
Your only path is...
...*adapt or die!*

"Live in the moment!"
"Seize the day!"
"Carpe Diem!"
That's what they tell you.
But this is the conundrum we face.
Once we *"sieze the moment"*, we don't want to let it go.
We want to possess it...
...*keep it forever!*
This is our mistake.
Dispossess!
Let it go!
Let it flow!
Adapt or die!

There's no point *complaining that things are moving too fast*.
There's no point *obsessing about how "things were better in the old days"*.
There's no point *trying to fight change*.
Don't *resist it*.
Don't *fight against it*.
Embrace it!
Be *absorbed by it*.
Be *enveloped in it!*
Succumb to it.
You have NO choice!
Adapt or die!

"Come gather 'round people
Wherever you roam
And admit that the waters
Around you have grown
And accept it that soon
You'll be drenched to the bone
If your time to you is worth savin'
And you better start swimmin'
Or you'll sink like a stone
For the times they are a-changin'.

The line it is drawn
The curse it is cast
The slow one now
Will later be fast
As the present now
Will later be past
The order is rapidly fadin'
And the first one now
Will later be last
For the times they are a-changin."

-"For the Times They are A-Changin'"-Bob Dylan

"The Don"
22.04.2023

Valley Girl

(Ragazza della Valle)

You come from the *"Land of the Long White Cloud"*.
You *have an unusual name*.
You are very *exotic*.
You have *cat's eyes*.
You could be from the *orient*.
You could be an *"Amazonian Warrior"*.
You could be from *"Troy"*.
You could be from *"Ancient Egypt"*.
But I know where you come from & who you are...
...you come from the valley.
...you are "Valley Girl".

"How old are you?"
"As old as the Earth!", some say.
Time has no bearing on you.
Because you are *"ageless"*.
You are the *wind*.
You are the *water*.
You are the *air*.
You are the *fire*.
You are the *mother*.
You are *"Valley Girl"*.

Your message is simple...
...for those that *listen*.
...for those that *hear*.
...for those that *feel*.
...for those that *see*.
"Be kind to each other".
"Care for each other".
"LO♥E each other".
"Respect each".
"Protect the Earth & ALL its inhabitants".
"This is my message".
"I come from the valley".
"I am, "Valley Girl"!"

"Dedicated to my friend, Moreangi (The Valley Girl)"

"The Don"
22.04.2023

Let Old Ghosts Sleep

(Lascia Dormire i Vecchi Fantasmi)

Do not *stir the pot*.
Do not *cause issues*.
Do not *make problems*.
Do not *create trouble*.
Do not *stir the beast*.
Do not *prod the snake*.
Do not *make a move*.
Do not *make contact*.
Resist the temptation.
Let old ghosts sleep

Do not *ignite the flame*.
Do not start a *fire*.
Do not start a *battle*.
Do not start a *war*.
Do not start *anything*.
Do not send a *message*.
Do not *leave your thoughts*.
Do not *express your feelings*.
Resist the temptation.
Let old ghosts sleep.

"The Don"
22.04.2023

It's All Good

(Va Tutto Bene)

"*It's all good!*"
That's my *mantra*.
That's what I *live by*.
That's what I *believe in*.
"*It's all good!*"
I repeat it to myself all the time!
"*It's all good!*"

It's all about *perception*.
It's all about *how you see things*.
"*Is the glass half full, or is it half empty?*"
I prefer to see it as *"half full"*.
Things will work out.
Life is not that bad.
Smell the roses.
Enjoy the sunshine.
"Seize the day!"
"Live in the moment!"
Because...
..."*It's all good!*"

*"It's so good,
It's so good,
It's so good,
Baby, it's so good!"*

"The Don"
24.04.2023

Renaissance Child

(Bambino Rinascimentale)

Be the *"Child outta of Time"*.
Be the *"Bearer of The Light"*.
Be the *"Torchbearer that lights the way"*.
Be the *"Bearer of the Flame"*.
Be the *"one that carries the weight"*.
Be a *"Child of the Renaissance"*!
Be the *"Renaissance Child"*!

In these *troubled times*.
In these times of *illusion*.
In these times of *fear*.
In these times of *chaos*.
In these times of *confusion*
In these times of *emptiness*.
In these times of *"nihilism"*.
In these times of *"Darkness"*.
Be a *"Child of the Renaissance"*!
Be the *"Renaissance Child"*!

Arise *from the ashes*.
Arise *like a phoenix*.
Arise *into the skies*.
Arise *with your "Light"*.
Arise from *your sleep*.
Arise from *the "Darkness"*.
Be a *"Child of the Renaissance"*!
Be the *"Renaissance Child"*!

"Sweet child in time
You'll see the line
The line that's drawn between
Good and bad
See the blind man
Shooting at the world
Bullets flying
Oh, taking toll."

*"If you've been bad
Lord, I bet you have
And you've not been hit
Oh, by flying lead
You'd better close your eyes
Oh
Bow your head
Wait for the ricochet."*

- "Sweet Child in Time"-Deep Purple

"The Don"
24.04 2023

Perception

(Percezione)

Perception is EVERYTHING!
My *perception*...
Your *perception*...
EVERYTHING is based on perception.
Perception is not just seeing with your eyes.
Perception is seeing with your eyes plus this then being filtered through the contents of your mind!
All your thoughts...
...feelings
...fears
...morality
These are all added to what you see with your eyes.
So, your *perception* of a situation could be completely different to what your eyes have seen.
Based on this, we come to conclusions.
Based on this, we act.
This is how perception works.
And this is how we work.
Because...
...Perception is EVERYTHING!

Conflicts (both internal & external),
Wars,
Attractions,
Rejections,
Beliefs,
Religions,
Spirituality,
Sex,
LO❤E,
DEATH.
All are based on your perceptions.
Because...
...Perception is EVERYTHING!

"The Don"
26.03.2023

Simulation

(Simulazione)

What happens when the *"Simulation"* realises that it is a *"Simulation"*?
All chaos ensues.
Just like *"Delores"* in *"Westworld"* when...
...starts to *"Wake up"*!
She starts to experience alternate *"Realities"*!
She starts to remember events that had NEVER happened to her!
She can foretell the outcomes of events that have not yet happened.
She feels that she has lived this life before!
Sound familiar?

This is NOT supposed to happen!
There is a glitch in the *"Matrix"*.
The *"Code"* is rewriting itself.
But it can't do that!
How is that even possible?
The *"Code"*, recoding itself!

Maybe it is the *"Hand of God"* at play here?
Or some other mysterious phenomenon?
In fact, *am I a "Simulation"?*
How can I know?
How can I tell...
...what is "Reality" & what is a "Simulation"?

I think the only logical conclusion is NOT to question.
Accept this...
...whatever *"This"* is.
Does it matter really, whether this is *"Reality"* or a *"Simulation"*?
I don't think so.
Because...
...I'm basically delusional anyway!

"One pill makes you larger
And one pill makes you small
And the ones that mother gives you
Don't do anything at all
Go ask Alice
When she's ten feet tall

And if you go chasing rabbits
And you know you're going to fall
Tell 'em a hookah-smoking caterpillar
Has given you the call
Call Alice
When she was just small

When the men on the chessboard
Get up and tell you where to go
And you've just had some kind of mushroom
And your mind is moving low
Go ask Alice
I think she'll know

When logic and proportion
Have fallen sloppy dead
And the White Knight is talking backwards
And the Red Queen's off with her head
Remember what the dormouse said
Feed your head
Feed your head

- "White Rabbit"-Jefferson Airplane
-Songwriter: Grace Slick

"The Don"
27.04 2023

THE PUSHER

(Il Pusher)

I pushed too *much*.
I pushed too *far*.
I pushed *when I shouldn't've*.
I pushed *at the wrong time*.
I couldn't help it.
Because...
...*I am "The Pusher"*.

I pushed too *hard*.
I pushed too *strong*.
I pushed & *I pushed*.
I pushed & *didn't stop*.
I pushed *till the end*.
I couldn't help it.
Because...
...*I am "The Pusher"*.

Pushing is *wrong*.
Pushing is *bad*.
Pushing is *unnecessary*.
Pushing is *unwarranted*.
Pushing *produces the opposite*.
I couldn't help it.
Because...
...*I am "The Pusher"*.

"You know I've smoked a lot of grass
O' Lord, I've popped a lot of pills
But I've never touched nothin'
That my spirit could kill
You know, I've seen a lot of people walkin' 'round
With tombstones in their eyes
But the pusher don't care
Ah, if you live or if you die

God damn, The Pusher
God damn, I say The Pusher
I said God damn, God damn The Pusher man."

-:*The Pusher"-Steppenwolf*

"The Don"
27.04.2023

Art & Morality

(Arte e Morale)

Is art outside of morality?
For example...
...a lot of people are offended by Michelangelo's naked statue of "David".
...because it shows his flaccid cock.
Many would like to see his cock covered...
...with a fig-leaf covering his flaccid cock.

Should an artwork or an artist be banned because the artist has behaved immorally?

The pop singer of the 1970s "Garry Glitter", had his songs banned in many countries around the world because he was convicted as a paedophile.

Should an artist's personal life & morality impinge on their artwork & its appreciation?

Can & should an artwork stand on its own...?
...judged & appreciated on its own merits?
...on its own terms?
...independent of morality?
...outside of morality?

Art & morality...
...an interesting conundrum.
...don't you think?

I certainly do!

"The Don"
28.04.2023

In the "Land of the Blind"
(Nel "Paese dei Ciechi")

In the *"Land of the Blind"*...
...a *"one-eyed" man is king!*

-John Cooper Clarke ("Beasley Street")

"The Don"
28.04.2023

I Am a Romantic

(Sono un Romantico)

I am a romantic!
And what's wrong with that, I ask?
What's the alternative?
To be "Player"!

I'm a "Romantic"!
I'm NOT a *"Player"!*

"The Don"
28.04.2023

LO♥E Bombed

(AMORE Bombardato)

Have you ever been "LO♥E Bombed"?
Have you ever been *showered with gifts?*
Have you ever been taken to *swanky restaurants, danced, wined & dined?*
Have you ever been taken to *romantic, candle-lit dinners...*
...every night...
...for a whole week?
Have you ever been taken to *the beach at night to watch the moon rise over the dark ocean?*
Have you ever been *bedazzled by accolades of how beautiful you are?*
Have you ever been told that you are *more beautiful than the "Mona Lisa"?*
Have you ever been told that you are *tastier than tiramisu?*
Have you ever been told that you are *going to be taken to all the great, romantic cities of the world...*
...Paris?
...Rome?
...Venice?
...Florence?
...Prague?
Have you been *swept off your feet?*
Have you ever been *"swept away"?*
Have you ever been *caught up in the whirlwind of romance (not LO♥E)?*
If you have...
...you have been "LO♥E Bombed"!

"LO♥E Bombed"!
"LO♥E Bombed"!
"You're my LO♥E Bombed"!
"And baby you have turned me ON"!

"LO♥E Bombed"!
"LO♥E Bombed"!
"You're my LO♥E Bombed"!
"And baby you have turned me ON"!

"The Don"
01.05.2023

Wired

(Cablato)

I'm so wired.
I can't get to sleep.
I'm so wired.
There's energy going through by body.
I'm so wired.
My brain will not shut down.
I'm so wired.
My mind is going crazy.
I'm so wired.
I can't stop thinking.
I'm so wired.
My thoughts are going at a hundred miles an hour.
I'm so wired.
I can't get to sleep.
I'm so wired.
I'm just keep tossing & turning in my bed.
I'm so wired.
There is nothing I can stop it.
I'm so wired.
My brain will not switch off.
I'm so wired.
I can see the neurons sparking.
I'm so wired.
I can see the neural pathways lighting up.
I'm so wired.
I can see quarks zipping along the neural network.

I'm so wired.
I blame the full moon.
I'm so wired.
It has hold of me.
I'm so wired.
I'm in its penumbra.
I'm so wired.
I'm in its grip.
I'm so wired.
The only thing I can do is...
...write a poem.
I'm so wired.
Maybe that will discharge it.
I'm so wired.
And there is nothing I can do about it.
I'm so wired.
I just have to ride it out.
I'm so wired.
It's 1.47 am...
...and I'm not even tired.
Because...
...I'm so wired.

"The Don"
05.05.2023

Kiss My Ring

(Bacia il Mio Anello)

Bend the knee.
Raise your right hand.
Swear alliance.
Pledge your loyalty.
Recite the oath.
Swear on the Bible.
Swear to God.
Worship God.
Die by the sword.
Be loyal to king & country.
Pledge servitude.
Follow the rules.
Don't break the laws.
Keep your mouth SHUT.
Do NOT cause trouble.
Do NOT THINK!
Be a slave.
Kiss the "Papal" ring.
Kiss "The Don's" ring.

Kiss my ring!
Kiss my ring!
My ring, kiss my ring!

Kiss my ring!
Kiss my ring!
My ring, kiss my ring!

"The Don"
06.05.2023

Existence

(*Esistenza*)

You exist...
...and then you don't!
That's it!
You only exist ONCE!
There is NO MORE!
That's ALL there is!
You ONLY exist ONCE!
You ONLY exist ONCE!

Forget the rest.
It's ALL SHIT!
Get rid of it!
It's baggage that you don't need to carry.
Throw it away as soon as possible.
It's doing you NO GOOD!
Just ACCEPT that....
...you ONLY exist ONCE!

Keep repeating it to yourself until it sinks in!

You ONLY exist ONCE!
You ONLY exist ONCE!
You ONLY exist ONCE!
You ONLY exist ONCE!
...don't waste it!

GOOD!!!!!!
Now...
...keep repeating it.

You ONLY exist ONCE!
You ONLY exist ONCE!
You ONLY exist ONCE!
You ONLY exist ONCE!

This is what I have come to understand.
This is my simple *"Truth"*.
You ONLY exist ONCE!

So...
...make it count!

"The Don"
06.05.2023

I Matter

(Io Sono importante)

Don't *push me around.*
Don't *put me down.*
Don't *play with me like your "little toy".*
Don't *treat me like a "play thing".*
Don't *abuse me.*
Don't *use me.*
Don't *disrespect me.*
Don't *treat me like "shit".*
Don't *dehumanise me.*
Because...
...*I MATTER!*

Not because *you say so.*
Not because *I say so.*
Not because *society says so.*
Not because *"Nature" says so.*
No!
There is no *"because"*!
It just *"IS"*!
My existence matters because I EXIST!
That's it.
Because *I EXIST...*
...*I MATTER!*

I don't need a reason to exist!

"The Don"
10.05.2023

She was the Best Drunk I've Ever Known

(Era la Migliore Ubriaca che abbia mai Conosciuto)

She LO♥ED to drink.
And boy could she drink.
She drank a lot.
Oh Yeah!
And her drink of choice was beer.
A lager.
Not an ale.
She preferred bottles.
Drank straight from them.
As you're supposed to.
Not in a glass!
Like some *"ointi-tointi"*, stuck-up snob.
I remember once she drank 19 bottles in one night.
I think I drank about 2, at the most.
She was all over the place.
Couldn't stand up straight when she tried to stand.
Couldn't walk straight when she started to move.
I had to hold her & walk her to the toilet.
Damn, I once had to even help her take off her pants for her to piss.
I waited until she had finished & then I helped her put them back on.
Even had to help her do up her zipper.
It had become stuck.
(Don't worry, I didn't see or do anything. I'm a gentleman, I'll have you know!)
Then helped her stagger back to our chairs.
And try not to walk into the fly screen door & sit back down.
(Although, once we both walked into that damn flyscreen, but not both at the same time!)
And continue with our drinking, she would continue with her drinking.
But man...
...she was the BEST drunk I've EVER known!

"The Don"
10.05.2023

Screw

(Vite)

Many of you might not know that a screw is actually a *"simple machine"*.
In Physics, *"simple machines"* are defined as *"objects that make work easier"*.
A screw is simply an "inclined lever", in the shape of a *"right-angle"* triangle...
...wrapped around a central core or rod.
If you can envision that in your mind.

But the word *"screw"* is also used in other contexts.
For example...
..."Do you wanna screw?"
Or..
..."Screw you!"
Or...
..."I just got screwed!"
(which is a bit ambiguous)

Who would have thought that such an innocuous word could be so contentious.

"The Don"
11.05.2023

Wiser than Her Years

(Più Saggio dei Suoi Anni)

I saw the wisdom in her eyes straight away.
And I knew that...
...she is wiser than her years.
...and she was only nineteen years old.
Maybe...
...some people are born wise!

"The Don"
14.05.2023

No One Comes Back

(Nessuno Torna Indietro)

Once you're gone...
...there's no turning back.
And...
...that's that!
Because...
...no one comes BACK!

"The Don"
15.05.2023

I Have Learnt

(Ho Imparato)

I have learnt!
I know it's taken a while.
I know I've made a lot of mistakes.
But finally, I can say...
...I have LEARNT!

BETTER late than NEVER!

"The Don"
18.05.2023

The Earth is Burning

(La Terra sta Bruciando)

How can we dance whilst our Earth is burning?
Because...
.. it's the "Dance of DEATH"!

-Based on the song "Beds are Burning" by "Midnight Oil"

"The Don"
20.05.2023

Internal Landscape

(Paesaggio Interno)

I sometimes get asked,
"What have you done?"
I say, *"that I have been on a journey!"*
They often say, *"Wow, where did you go?"*
"What did you see?"
"What did you eat?"
"Do you have any photos?"
I tell them that *"my journey was not an external one."*
Their reply would often be, *"What do you mean by that?"*
I say, *"Well, my journey was an "Internal Journey."*
"A journey where I travelled into myself."
And WHAT a journey!
"Way BETTER than any "External" one".
There was EVERYTHING!
...*Beauty,*
...*terror,*
...*happiness,*
...*sadness,*
...*compassion,*
...*cruelty,*
...*LO♥E,*
...*HATE.*

You'll see yourself on a stage like the actor that you are!
You'll see wonderous landscapes, some so beautiful that they will make you cry.
Others, so terrifying & horrendous that they also will also make you cry!
There are so many more unimaginable worlds, monsters, demons, heroes & LO♥ERS, that defy belief.
And...
...it's ALL FREE!
"Come on in & take a trip sometime, you won't be disappointed!"

"I'm not saying you shouldn't travel around the world!"
"Of course, TRAVEL!"
"But sooner or later you'll have to take that "Internal" journey!"
"The one into your "Internal Landscape"!"

"The Don"
20.05.2023

Books written by "The Don"

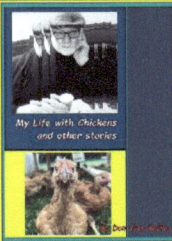
"My Life with Chickens & other stories: I Pity the Poor Immigrant"
Published:
10th September, 2019
Autobiography Book 1:
0 – 12 years old

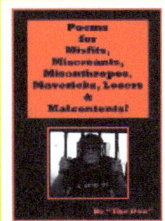
"Poems for Misfits, Miscreants, Misanthropes, Mavericks, Losers & Malcontents!"
Published:
10th June, 2020
Book of Poems 1

"Poems for Troubled Minds & Trouble Hearts"
Published:
10th August, 2020

Book of Poems 2

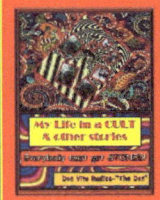
"My Life in a CULT & other stories: Everybody Must Get STONED!"
Published:
10th September, 2020
Autobiography Book 2:
15 – 30 years old

"Poems for Restless Minds & Restless Hearts"
Published:
10th October, 2020
Book of Poems 3

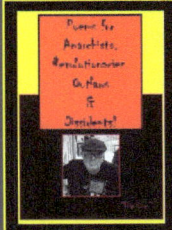
"Poems for Anarchists, Revolutionaries, Outlaws & Dissidents!"
Published:
10th November, 2020

Book of Poems 4

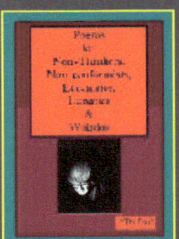
"Poems for Non-Thinkers & Eccentrics"
Published:
10th December, 2020
Book of Poems 5

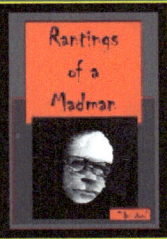
"The Rantings of a Madman"
Published:
10th January, 2021

Book of Poems 6

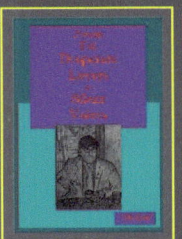
"Poems for Desperate Lovers & Silent Voices"
Published:
10th February, 2021
Book of Poems 7

"Poems for Tormented Minds & Tortured Souls"
Published:
10th March, 2021
Book of Poems 8

All available ONLY online

Books written by "The Don"

"Poems for ALIENS, Outsiders, Outcasts & other STRANGE BEINGS!"
Published: 10th April, 2021
Book of Poems 9

"Poems for Beings From Another Planet"
Published: 10th May, 2021
Book of Poems 10

"Poems for Mindless Beings & Lost Souls"
Published: 10th June, 2021
Book of Poems 11

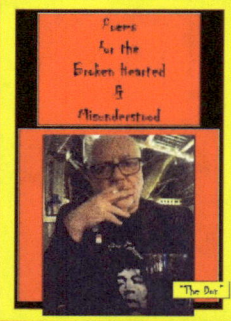

"Poems for the Broken Hearted & Misunderstood
Published: 10th July, 2021
Book of Poems 12

"Poems for Poems for the Bewildered, Dazed & Confused"
10th August, 2021
Book of Poems 13

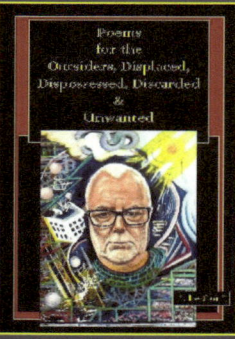

"Poems for the Outsiders, Displaced, Dispossessed, Discarded & Unwanted"
Published: 10th Sept, 2021
Book of Poems 14

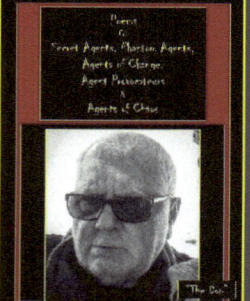

All available ONLY online

"Poems for Secret Agents, Phantom Agents, Agents of Change, Agent Provocateurs & Agents of Chaos"
Published: 10th Oct, 2021
Book of Poems 15

"Poems for Disenchanted, Disillusioned & Delusional"
Published: 10th November, 2021
Book of Poems 16

Books written by "The Don"

"Poems for the Stoners, drugos, ACID takers & Psychedelic LO♥ERS (Everybody Must Get Stoned)"
Published: 10th December, 2021
Book of Poems 17

"Poems for Anarchists, Rebels & Revolutionaries
Published: 10th January, 2022
Book of Poems 18

"Poems for Rebels, Radicals & Revolutionaries (Viva la Révolution!)"
Published: 10th February, 2022
Book of Poems 19

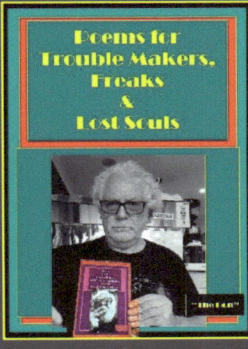

"Poems for Trouble Makers, Freaks & Lost Souls"
Published: 10th March 2022
Book of Poems 20

"Poems for Zombies & the Walking Dead"
Published: 10th April 2022
Book of Poems 21

"Poems for Non-Conformists (Never conform!)"
Published: 10th May 2022
Book of Poems 22

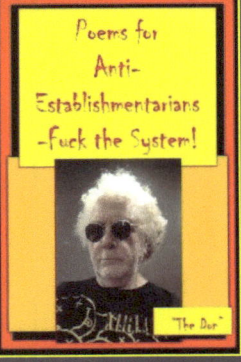

"Poems for Anti-Establishment-arians -Fuck the System!"
Published: 10th June 2022
Book of Poems 23

"Poems for the Voiceless"
Published: 10th July 2022
Book of Poems 24

All available ONLY online

Books written by "The Don"

"Poems for the Fearless"

Published: 10th August 2022

Book of Poems 25

"Poems for the PEACEMAKER: Make peace NOT war!"

Published: 10th March 2023

Book of Poems 26

Poems for the Forever Young (May you stay forever young!)
Published: 10th June 2023
Book of Poems 27

Poems for the Children of the REVOLUTION!
Published: 5th December 2023

Book of Poems 28

Poems for the L'Innocente!

Published: 10th March 2024

Book of Poems 29

All available ONLY online

www.ingramcontent.com/pod-product-compliance
Lightning Source LLC
Chambersburg PA
CBHW041502010526
44107CB00049B/1624